DESTINATION MARS

LANDING ON
MARS

Margaret J. Goldstein

Lerner Publications ◆ Minneapolis

Lerner Publications Company
An imprint of Lerner Publishing Group, Inc.
241 First Avenue North
Minneapolis, MN 55401 USA

For reading levels and more information, look up this title at www.lernerbooks.com.

Main body text set in Aptifer Sans LT Pro.
Typeface provided by Linotype AG.

Designer: Viet Chu

Library of Congress Cataloging-in-Publication Data

Names: Goldstein, Margaret J., author.
Title: Landing on Mars / Margaret J. Goldstein.
Description: Minneapolis, MN, USA : Lerner Publications Company, an imprint
    of Lerner Publishing Group, Inc., [2024] | Series: Destination Mars. Alternator
    books | Includes bibliographical references and index. | Summary: "Conditions
    on Mars make landing there very challenging. Readers get a close-up look at
    these challenges, plus information on how scientists have successfully landed
    rovers on Mars and how they might land humans there someday"— Provided by
    publisher.
Identifiers: LCCN 2022034615 (print) | LCCN 2022034616 (ebook) |
    ISBN 9781728490649 (library binding) | ISBN 9781728496863 (ebook)
Subjects: LCSH: Space vehicles—Landing—Mars (Planet) —Juvenile literature. |
    Mars (Planet) —Exploration—Juvenile literature.
Classification: LCC TL799.M3 G65 2024 (print) | LCC TL799.M3 (ebook) |
    DDC 629.45/53—dc23/eng/20221004

LC record available at https://lccn.loc.gov/2022034615
LC ebook record available at https://lccn.loc.gov/2022034616

Manufactured in the United States of America
1-52995-51013-11/29/2022

TABLE OF CONTENTS

New York City's Empire State Building lit red in February 2021 to celebrate Mars 2020's arrival at the Red Planet.

SEVEN MINUTES OF TERROR

The scientists were quiet. They listened as a mission controller reported on an event taking place 127 million miles (204 million km) away. On this day, February 18, 2021, the spacecraft Mars 2020, carrying the Perseverance rover, was about to land on Mars.

Scientists at the US National Aeronautics and Space Administration (NASA) had spent years planning this mission. Mars 2020 launched on July 30, 2020. As the craft sped toward Mars, scientists on Earth controlled it with radio signals. They adjusted its computers and other equipment to keep the spacecraft on course and working properly.

PREPARE FOR LANDING

Mars 2020 reached Mars after nearly seven months of travel. But landing on the Red Planet would be tricky. It takes about seven minutes for a spacecraft to descend from the top of Mars's atmosphere to the planet's surface. Usually, it takes much longer for radio signals to travel from Mars to Earth and back again. Because of the time lag, scientists cannot control the spacecraft by radio as it lands. During these seven minutes of terror, they can only wait.

As Mars 2020 descended, the NASA scientists watched their monitors. At last, the mission controller confirmed the spacecraft had safely touched down on the surface. The scientists cheered and jumped from their seats. The seven minutes of terror were over. Perseverance could begin exploring Mars.

Because it is so difficult to accomplish, landing on Mars is a cause for celebration.

CHAPTER 1

THE PLANET NEXT DOOR

Mars is one of Earth's nearest neighbors. Since ancient times, humans have been curious about the Red Planet. In the late twentieth century, NASA and other space agencies began sending unpiloted missions to Mars. Some of these spacecraft are still operating, exploring Mars and sending information to Earth via radio signals.

Some spacecraft orbit the planet. They take photos, make maps of the planet's surface, study Martian weather, and measure radiation and other energy on Mars. To study Mars up close, scientists have landed rovers on the Martian surface. The rovers hold scientific instruments that collect soil and rock samples, take up-close photos, detect chemicals in the air, and look for water and other substances underground.

Some of the active spacecraft exploring Mars are from NASA, while others are from Europe, China, the United Arab Emirates, and India.

QUESTIONS AND ANSWERS

Landers give scientists valuable information about Mars. Each day since the first successful Mars landing, we have learned much about the Red Planet. Mars missions

Mars is a dry planet, but billions of years ago, it was watery.

Billions of years ago, Mars may have looked something like this.

have taught us that about four billion years ago, Mars was much warmer. It was also a watery planet, with rivers, lakes, and seas.

Was Mars home to living things when it was warm and watery? Perseverance is trying to find out. It is looking for signs of ancient life on Mars. Future space missions will look for answers to other questions.

A rocket carrying the Mars 2020 Perseverance rover launches on July 30, 2020.

Engineers thoroughly clean spacecraft before launch. They remove microbes and other substances from Earth that might contaminate the results of scientific experiments.

When NASA's Viking 1 lander took the first color photographs on Mars's surface, scientists discovered that sunrises and sunsets on Mars appear blue.

CHAPTER 2

INTO THE MARTIAN ATMOSPHERE

How do you land a rover on Mars? The Mars 2020 mission used advanced technology. A spacecraft made of multiple parts took off from Earth. One part, the cruise stage, held all the equipment needed for the journey through space, such as fuel tanks and rocket engines.

When the spacecraft reached Mars, it no longer needed the cruise stage. Before the spacecraft descended into the Martian atmosphere, the cruise stage separated from the rest of the craft.

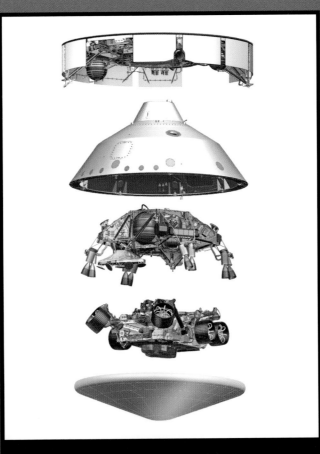

This illustration shows each part of the Perseverance lander. *Top to bottom*: the cruise stage, back shell, descent stage, rover, and heat shield.

The rest of the spacecraft then entered the atmosphere, traveling at 12,500 miles (20,000 km) per hour. As it zoomed downward, the spacecraft rubbed against gases in the atmosphere. This rubbing created friction, which slowed the craft. The friction also created intense heat, as high as 2,370°F (1,300°C). The spacecraft had a heat shield that could withstand high temperatures. It kept the rest of the craft from burning up.

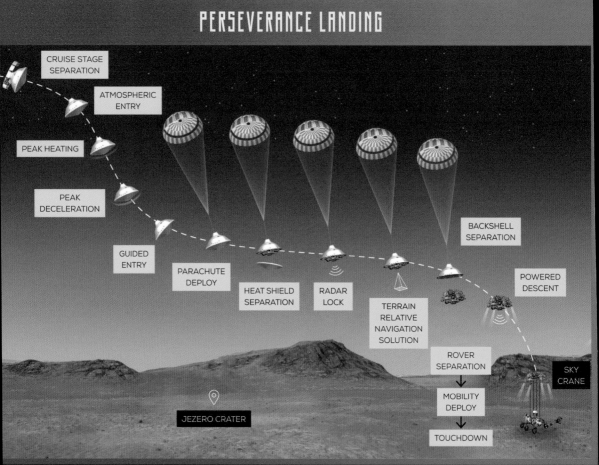

PERSEVERANCE LANDING

CRUISE STAGE SEPARATION

ATMOSPHERIC ENTRY

PEAK HEATING

PEAK DECELERATION

GUIDED ENTRY

PARACHUTE DEPLOY

HEAT SHIELD SEPARATION

RADAR LOCK

TERRAIN RELATIVE NAVIGATION SOLUTION

BACKSHELL SEPARATION

POWERED DESCENT

ROVER SEPARATION

MOBILITY DEPLOY

TOUCHDOWN

SKY CRANE

JEZERO CRATER

Engineers tested Perseverance's parachute by blasting it with winds that were twice as fast as the speed of sound.

GROUND GAME

About halfway through the descent, a giant parachute opened from the spacecraft's backshell. The parachute slowed the craft even more, to about 200 miles (320 km) per hour. The heat shield was no longer needed. It separated from the craft and fell to the ground.

As Mars 2020 neared its landing site, the backshell and the parachute separated from the spacecraft. Only two parts were left: the descent stage and the rover. The descent stage fired up retrorockets. These slowed the craft even more and moved it to its precise landing spot. Finally, at a speed of about 1.7 miles (2.7 km) per hour, the descent stage carefully lowered the Perseverance rover on cables until it rested on the ground. The rover cut the cables, and the descent stage flew off and landed nearby. Perseverance was ready to begin exploring the surface of Mars.

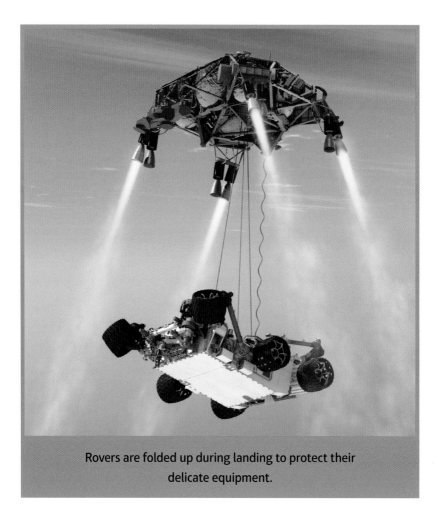

Rovers are folded up during landing to protect their delicate equipment.

SELF-DRIVING SPACECRAFT

New technology makes Mars landings safer and more precise than ever before. For instance, Mars 2020 used a computer system called terrain relative navigation. As the craft descended, it took pictures of the ground below, compared them to images on a human-made map, and figured out its exact location. Terrain relative navigation also allowed Mars 2020 to adjust its course to avoid obstacles like boulders, ensuring a safe landing.

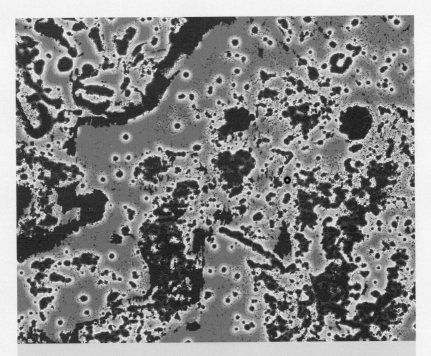

Using the terrain relative navigation system, Perseverance marked parts of Mars's surface as unsafe (*in red*) and safe (*in blue*) for landing.

The Martian surface is extremely rocky.

CHAPTER 3

SUCCESSES AND FAILURES

Mars landings are filled with challenges. The Martian atmosphere is one of them. The atmosphere is thin—the gas particles are very spread out. When a spacecraft descends, it rubs against the gas particles. But the particles are too spread out to slow the craft to a speed that's safe for landing. When designing a Mars mission, space scientists have to equip vehicles with big parachutes, powerful retrorockets, and other gear for extra slowing power.

Many places on Mars are rocky. They have cliffs, craters, and boulders. Mission planners usually choose flat and smooth landing spots. But Mars also has strong winds and dust storms that can blow a craft off course or damage it during landing. During the seven minutes of terror, scientists worry about spacecraft landing in the wrong spot or crashing into rocks and other hazards.

The Perseverance rover on its Mars mission

Scientists consider all these dangers when planning a mission. But even with the best planning, some landings fail.

LESSONS LEARNED

Space agencies from many countries have sent spacecraft to Mars. Some missions have succeeded, but many have failed. Some failures took place in outer space or even as vehicles left Earth. Other failures happened on landing.

Perseverance's backshell was destroyed when it hit the ground, but the rover no longer needed to use it.

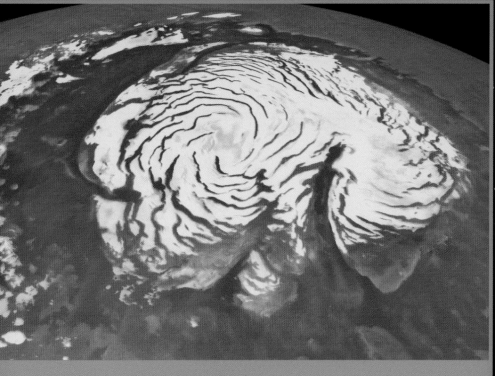

Mars's polar region

NASA's Mars Polar Lander was a failure. Designed to look for frozen water near the planet's south pole, the spacecraft reached Mars in December 1999. Due to a software error, its retrorockets shut down too soon during landing. The craft hit the Martian surface at 50 miles (80 km) per hour and broke apart. Software errors also doomed Schiaparelli, a 2016 European Space Agency mission. During landing, the craft's onboard computers released the backshell and fired the retrorockets at the wrong time. The spacecraft smashed into the ground at 335 miles (540 km) per hour.

Multiple giant airbags protected Spirit and Opportunity as they bounced to a halt on Mars's surface.

Space scientists learn from their failures, but each mission poses new challenges. To land the rovers Spirit in 2003 and Opportunity in 2004, NASA scientists encased them in giant airbags. The bags bounced several times when they hit the Martian surface. The rovers, cushioned safely inside, were not harmed. NASA couldn't use airbags to land the Curiosity rover in 2012 because it was too big and heavy. So scientists devised a new system, lowering the rover on cables. The Curiosity landing went smoothly, so scientists used a similar process to land Perseverance in 2021.

ON THE ROCKS

When planning a Mars mission, scientists usually choose a landing spot that's free of boulders, cliffs, and other obstacles. But for the Perseverance landing, they did the opposite. They chose Jezero Crater, a rocky site that was once a watery lake. Why? Because the rover's mission is to look for signs of ancient life on Mars. Scientists think an ancient lake bed is one of the most likely places to find them.

An illustration of NASA's Perseverance rover exploring inside Mars's Jezero Crater

CHAPTER 4

LANDING WITH HUMANS

People have long dreamed of visiting Mars. Humans on Mars
could do experiments, explore the terrain, and learn about
the Red Planet. But landing humans on Mars will be very
challenging.

On the positive side, humans on a Mars mission could help steer the craft during landing. They could adjust onboard computers and other equipment to fix problems. They could make sure the parachutes, retrorockets, and other landing gear worked properly. But if something went wrong and the craft crashed, the space travelers would probably be killed.

Once landed, humans on Mars could run new kinds of experiments and repair broken rovers.

Humans on Mars will need shelters to protect them from radiation and extremely cold temperatures. They will need equipment for creating oxygen, running experiments, and communicating with Earth. They will need food, fuel, space suits, and more.

Mission planners probably wouldn't try to land this equipment all at once. The load would be too heavy. A heavy

If humans reach Mars, they will need shelters to protect them from dangerous radiation.

The International Space Station orbits Earth. One day a similar station might orbit Mars.

craft is very hard to slow as it lands. Instead, planners might send equipment in a big cargo spaceship. Then they could send down small loads from the big ship, one at a time.

COMPLETING THE TRIP

Even if humans were to land and explore successfully on Mars, a challenge remains: How do the space travelers get back to Earth? They would start out in a Mars ascent vehicle. This small craft would take off from the Martian surface. It would meet up with a larger craft orbiting Mars, which would fly the travelers home.

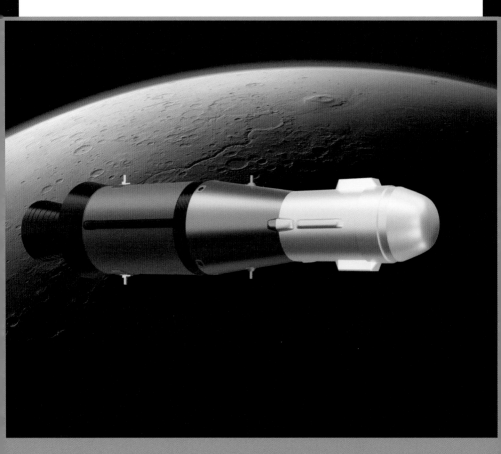

An illustration of NASA's Mars Ascent Vehicle

This illustration shows how tubes containing rock and soil samples may one day be launched from Mars.

Mars landings aren't easy. Taking off from Mars won't be easy either. Can it be done? Only time will tell.

Glossary

atmosphere: the layer of gases surrounding a planet

descend: to move downward

friction: a force created when objects rub against each other, causing them to slow, creating heat

heat shield: an outer covering designed to protect a spacecraft from high temperatures

orbit: to travel around a planet or another body in space

oxygen: a gas that humans and other living things need to survive

radiation: powerful energy that travels through space and can be deadly to living things

Red Planet: a nickname for Mars. Mars is reddish because its soil contains a lot of iron.

retrorocket: a small rocket that pushes against the motion of a vehicle, causing it to slow

rover: a wheeled vehicle equipped with cameras and other instruments, designed to explore the surface of a planet

Learn More

Cohn, Jessica. *Mars Rovers*. New York: Children's Press, 2022.

Exploring Mars
https://www.timeforkids.com/g56/exploring-mars-2/?rl=en-800

Hamilton, John. *Mars Landers*. Minneapolis: Abdo & Daughters, 2019.

Hirsch, Rebecca E. *Mysteries of Mars*. Minneapolis: Lerner Publications, 2021.

Kenney, Karen Latchana. *Cutting-Edge Journey to Mars*. Minneapolis: Lerner Publications, 2020.

The Mars Rovers
https://spaceplace.nasa.gov/mars-rovers/en/ama

Mission to Mars!
https://www.mensaforkids.org/teach/lesson-plans/mission-to-mars/

Index

Photo Acknowledgments

Image credits: NASA/Emma Howells, p. 4; Bill Ingalls/NASA/Getty Images, p. 5;
Stockbym/NASA/Alamy Stock Photo, p. 6; NASA, pp. 7, 8, 9, 10, 12, 13, 14, 15,
16, 22, 25, 27, 28, 29; NASA/JPL/Lockheed Martin/Pat Corkery, p. 11; NASA/JPL-
Caltech, pp. 17, 18, 20, 23; Gerbil/Wikipedia, p. 19; NASA/JPL-Caltech/MSSS, p. 21;
dottedhippo/NASA/Getty Images, p. 24; Ana Aguirre Perez/Shutterstock, p. 26.
Design elements: ESA/DLR/FU-Berlin; Tiradae Manyum/EyeEm/Getty Images.

Cover: NASA/JPL-Caltech